My teeth

First published in 2011 by Wayland

Text copyright © Claire Llewellyn
Photograph copyright © Wayland
with the exception of graphic p16 © Istock
and image p19 © Thierry Berrod, Mona
Lisa Production/Science Photo Library

Wayland
338 Euston Road
London NW1 3BH

Wayland Australia
Level 17/207 Kent Street
Sydney, NSW 2000

Series Editor: Louise John
Editor: Katie Powell
Design: D.R.ink
Photographer: Andy Crawford
Consultant: Shirley Bickler

A CIP catalogue record for this book is
available from the British Library.

ISBN 9780750263801

Printed in China

Wayland is a division of Hachette
Children's Books,
an Hachette UK Company

www.hachette.co.uk

With thanks to the Oxfordshire Salaried
Primary Dental Surgery and Jenny
Slatter and Jake and Katherine Moss

Contents

My teeth

I have lots of teeth.

My teeth are hard
and white and strong.

They can really bite!

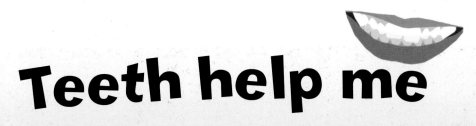

Teeth help me

My teeth help me to smile and talk.

They help me to eat.

Teeth and food

Front teeth

Back teeth

My teeth help me to eat my food.

My front teeth **bite** my food.

My back teeth **chew** it into bits.

9

Germs and teeth

My teeth have lots of germs on them.

The germs can make my teeth go bad. Then they get holes in them.

Mum says:
Bad teeth can hurt.

Brushing my teeth

Every day I brush my teeth to get rid of germs.

I wet my toothbrush...

Mum says:
Brush your teeth at least twice a day.

I put on some toothpaste...

...and I **brush**, **brush**, **brush!**

13

Sweet foods

Sweet foods are bad for my teeth.

Mum says:
Don't eat lots of sweet foods.

Fizzy drink

Sweets

Biscuits

Cakes

Chocolate

These foods are good.
They are not so sweet.

Fruit

Water

Seeds

Cheese

Breadsticks

15

At the dentist

Sometimes Mum takes me to the dentist.

Dentist

The dentist looks at my teeth.

Mum says:
A dentist helps you to look after your teeth.

Filling a tooth

If the dentist spots a hole in a tooth, she puts a filling in.

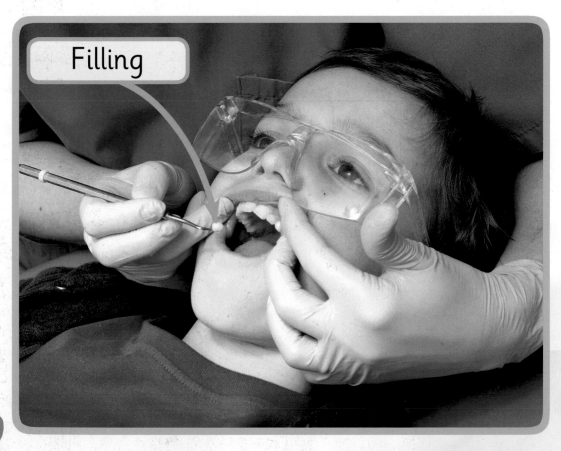

Filling

The filling helps to keep germs out.

Mum says:

Germs can make a big hole in your teeth.

These are the germs that live on your teeth.

Teeth for life

I look after my teeth. They are white and hard and strong.

They are going
to stay that way!

Mum says:
Teeth have to
last all your life.

21

Good or bad?

Which of these foods can you eat a lot of?

Biscuits

Breadsticks

Carrots

Cakes

Chocolate

Which of these foods are bad for your teeth?

Water

Fizzy drink

Fruit

Sweets

Seeds

Cheese

START READING is a series of highly enjoyable books for beginner readers. **The books have been carefully graded to match the Book Bands widely used in schools.** This enables readers to be sure they choose books that match their own reading ability.

Look out for the Band colour on the book in our Start Reading logo.

The Bands are:

Pink Band 1A & 1B

Red Band 2

Yellow Band 3

Blue Band 4

Green Band 5

Orange Band 6

Turquoise Band 7

Purple Band 8

Gold Band 9

START READING books can be read independently or shared with an adult. They promote the enjoyment of reading through satisfying stories and non-fiction narratives, which are supported supported by fun illustrations and photographs.

Claire Llewellyn has written many books for children. Some of them are about real things like animals and the Moon, others are storybooks. Claire has two children, but they are getting too big for her books now. She hopes you will enjoy reading them instead!